THE

MW00643869

Bart Tesoriero

Nihil Obstat: Right Reverend Archimandrite Francis Vivona, S.T.M., J.C.L.

Imprimatur: Most Reverend Joseph A. Pepe, D.D., J.C.D.

Date: June 11, 2010
               The Feast of the Sacred Heart of Jesus

Library of Congress Control Number: 2011962067
ISBN 1-936020-77-5

Copyright 2010 by Aquinas Press
Second Printing, January 2012

TABLE OF CONTENTS

Confirmation

Baptism

Holy
Communion

Reconciliation

Marriage

Anointing

Holy Orders

of the Sick

INTRODUCTION

"God wants only love and life, for all people at all times."
POPE BENEDICT XVI

My dad was from Brooklyn and my mother from Phoenix. When I graduated from high school, my parents sent me back East to meet my Dad's extended family. I was submerged in Italian culture from the moment I entered my grandparents' home and smelled the spaghetti sauce emanating from the kitchen! It was a homecoming to a place I'd never been before.

Many of us have been raised in the sacramental life of the Church, and perhaps have not stopped to reflect on the grace that surrounds us daily. Some of us have wandered away from our birthright, and, like the prodigal son, have "come to our senses" and returned to the faith of our parents and family.

From one perspective, sacraments are like going home again to a place where you are loved, fed, forgiven, and healed. They are meant to be healing, nurturing, life-giving encounters with God who has loved us from before the foundation of the world with an unconditional, personal love.

In this book we will explore the history, nature, rite, and effects of each of the seven sacraments of the Catholic Church. We will quote from the Scriptures, the *Catechism of the Catholic Church*, and the Documents of Vatican II. We pray that through this study of the sacraments you will come to feel more deeply in your heart the love God has just for you!

NEW WINE: FROM SPIRIT TO SACRAMENT

I came so that they might have life and have it more abundantly.
JOHN 10:10

Jesus came to give us LIFE—eternal, everlasting life—the life He Himself enjoyed in the bosom of the Father with the Holy Spirit from all eternity. When people encountered Jesus, they felt His power, His life. Jesus was truly a sign from heaven that God had not forgotten nor abandoned His people. Those who responded with faith received His very presence. They felt consoled, peaceful, joyful, and holy. But after Jesus ascended into heaven, how was this life to be transmitted? How do *we* receive this life, which is itself the Kingdom?

Upon reflection, I think we must answer that Christ Jesus shares His divine life with us in many ways. He is present in His Spirit; He is present in His Word; He is present in His Body the Church; He is present in our worship and praise, and He is present in one another. He has chosen through His Church to guarantee a way we will always be able to receive His grace, and that is through the sacraments.

"Sacraments are perceptible signs (words and actions) accessible to our human nature. By the action of Christ and the power of the Holy Spirit they make present efficaciously the grace that they signify" (*Catechism of the Catholic Church*—CCC–1084). In other words, a sacrament is a channel—a sign of grace—"by which divine life is dispensed to us" (CCC 1131).

Our Lord, who loves us, communicates His life and grace to us through the sacraments He instituted. "It is he who baptizes, he who acts in his sacraments in order to communicate the grace that each sacrament signifies. ... As fire transforms into itself everything it touches, so the Holy Spirit transforms into the divine life whatever is subjected to his power" (CCC 1127).

Most of us already know this good news, but we can always become more aware of its absolute wonder: **We are saved!** God, our Divine Father, has penetrated the darkness in this world with His Kingdom. Jesus has delivered us from the power of the evil one (thank God!). The Comforter has come! We are *more* than mighty conquerors, through Him who loved us.

What's more, our experience of salvation isn't confined to one act, such as our Baptism, or one grace-filled encounter, such as we might have felt in our First Communion. No, God has so much more for each of us! The Wedding banquet is just that: an exquisite and abundant feast of divine love!

> *Rejoice with Jerusalem and be glad because of her,*
> *all you who love her;*
> *Exult, exult with her,*
> *all you who were mourning over her!*
> *Oh, that you may suck fully*
> *of the milk of her comfort,*
> *That you may nurse with delight*
> *at her abundant breasts!*
> ISAIAH 66:10-11

The New Testament Greek word *mysterion* was later translated into two Latin words: *sacramentum* and *mysterium*. *Sacramentum* refers broadly to the outer dimension of a sacrament as a sign of grace, and *mysterium* concerns the interior, unseen action of grace that the sacrament imparts. *Sacramentum* also means oath, and as such it refers to the biblical idea of covenant. A sacrament **ratifies God's covenant** with us and **renews** it as well. Perhaps the best example is the Holy Eucharist. In this sacrament, Jesus seals His everlasting covenant with us *and* renews it by feeding us with His very Body and Blood!

The Church celebrates the seven sacraments as a priestly community, for each Christian is anointed at Baptism as priest, prophet, and king. Ordained priests actually administer each of the sacraments (except for Matrimony, where the ordinary ministers are the spouses themselves).

Just as we prepare for a visit from a relative or friend, so the Holy Spirit prepares us for every sacrament—every guaranteed encounter with God—by the Word of God and the gift of faith. Thus we welcome God's Word and receive the strength and graces signified by each sacrament.

"The purpose of the sacraments is to sanctify men, to build up the Body of Christ and, finally, to give worship to God" (CCC 1123). Each sacrament is given to bear fruit in our lives. This fruit is both an interior growth in intimacy and communion with God, as well as an exterior, or visible, growth in love for others and a witness to them.

As we grow in love, God can better use us to reach out to others and bring them His good news. Only God can regenerate a human soul, yet He wants to use *us* to prepare the ground, to sow His Word, and to water it with His love.

"The Church affirms that for believers the sacraments of the New Covenant are *necessary for salvation*. 'Sacramental grace' is the grace of the Holy Spirit, given by Christ and proper to each sacrament. The Spirit heals and transforms those who receive him by conforming them to the Son of God" (CCC 1129). It is necessary for us, the children of God, to encounter Him many times and in many ways. In this way we can enjoy a much fuller life now, and in the world to come, eternal life.

The Church has discerned from the Scriptures, Apostolic Tradition, and the prevalent teaching of the Fathers of the Church, that there are seven sacraments, all instituted by Christ. Even so, the sacraments as defined rituals, each with its own "matter and form," developed gradually in the Church. The personal experience and reflection of the Church as a whole—clergy and laity alike—has helped develop the sacraments into the rituals we experience today.

It can be said that Jesus gave us the sacraments from His wounded side, which is the fountain of sacramental life for His Bride, the Church. Jesus embraced His Passion and death so that each one of us can know and receive His love. Thus each sacrament is a visible sign of Christ's love for us and an opportunity to share love with Him again.

THE SACRAMENTS OF INITIATION

According to the grace of God given to me, like a wise master builder I laid a foundation, and another is building upon it. But each one must be careful how he builds upon it, for no one can lay a foundation other than the one that is there, namely, Jesus Christ.

1 CORINTHIANS 3:10-11

Jesus is the sacrament of God. Jesus makes God present in our world, a world that is both physical and spiritual, material and invisible, understandable and fascinatingly mysterious!

Jesus makes God present **to us and in us,** and this presence brings us life—full, abundant, overflowing LIFE! It is a life we absolutely need. As Saint Augustine says, we are merely beggars telling other beggars where we have found bread.

The Sacraments of Initiation are gifts of grace, won for us by Jesus on the Cross, that initiate us into the unbelievable intimacy of divine life. We who are human, limited, and prone to sin, are invited by the Holy Trinity—the Father, Son, and Holy Spirit—into the very life and communion they share right now, this very moment, and have shared from before the foundation of the world.

The Sacraments of Initiation are Baptism, Confirmation, and Holy Eucharist. **Baptism** is the gift of new life in Jesus; **Confirmation** is the gift of the power of the Holy Spirit; the **Holy Eucharist** is the inestimable gift of the Body and Blood, Soul and Divinity, of Jesus Christ, given for us and for the salvation of the whole world! Our initiation into Christ Jesus, into His life, and into His Church are accomplished by these three sacraments together.

Baptism, Confirmation, and the Holy Eucharist form a foundation within us, a spiritual footing, as it were, where we can stand secure in the knowledge that God is with us. Through them we first experience eternal life, which is, according to Pope Benedict XVI, "a new quality of existence, fully immersed in the love of God, that frees us from evil and death and places us in endless communion with all our brothers and sisters who participate in the same Love. Thus, eternity can already be present at the center of earthly and temporal life when the soul, through grace, is joined to God, its ultimate foundation."

THE SACRAMENT OF BAPTISM

*"Go, therefore, and make disciples of all nations, baptizing them
in the name of the Father, and of the Son, and of the holy Spirit,
teaching them to observe all that I have commanded you.
And behold, I am with you always, until the end of the age."*

MATTHEW 28:19-20

Everything created has a beginning. In fact, the Bible itself
opens with these timeless words: "In the beginning God
created the heavens and the earth" (GENESIS 1:1–RSV, CATHOLIC
EDITION). Thus it follows that every human being also has a
beginning, in the awesome mystery of conception, as the
fertilized egg begins to grow into a child.

When our first parents, Adam and Eve, sinned by disobeying God, they lost sanctifying grace—the life of God within their souls. Their personal sin passed on as a deprivation of grace to all humans after them, with the exception of Jesus, the Son of God, and Mary, His mother, who was conceived without sin. This wounding of our human nature and weakening of our natural powers is called Original Sin.

God so loved the world, and each of us *personally*, that He gave His only Son—not just a gift, not just a blessing, but all He had to give—to ransom us, to take away our sin, and to give us everlasting life. God could not have done more for us.

Baptism, then, is the sacrament whereby Jesus, acting through the person who baptizes, cleanses us of Original Sin, gives us new life by making us a new creation, incorporates us into Himself, and makes us a member of His Body, the Church. Baptism infuses us with sanctifying grace, bestows upon us the gifts of the Holy Spirit, and empowers us with the theological virtues of faith, hope, and charity!

According to the *Catechism of the Catholic Church*, Baptism takes away original sin, all personal sins, and remits all punishment due to sin. Baptism brings us into the life of the Trinity—the Father, Son, and Holy Spirit—through sanctifying grace. "The faithful who by Baptism are incorporated into Christ, are placed in the People of God, and in their own way share the priestly, prophetic, and kingly office of Christ" (*Lumen Gentium*, 31).

A *priest* is a mediator, and thus Christ Jesus is the one mediator between God and man. Through Baptism we too can intercede for others and offer, with the ordained priesthood, the sacrifice of Jesus in the Eucharist, for as Saint Peter writes: "You are 'a chosen race, a royal priesthood ...'" (1 PETER 2:9).

A *prophet* is one who speaks the word of God, someone sent by God to bring His message to His people. Our Baptism gives us the authority and the anointing to proclaim the prophetic word of God to others, especially at home, school, and in the marketplace, through our words and example. As has been said, "We may be the only Bible someone ever reads."

A *king* is someone who governs. As subjects of the King of Kings, we govern by serving. God gives to the hierarchy—the pope, bishops, and priests—the grace and authority to govern the Church. He gives to the laity the grace and authority to serve one another. Parents, for instance, are called to the right ordering of their families, through their love and discipline. CEOs are called to the right ordering of their companies, by caring for their employees and delivering products of integrity.

Baptism imprints on the soul an indelible character: an invisible, permanent, and unrepeatable mark, which consecrates us for worship. We are forever changed as new creations, and that is why a person can receive Baptism only once. As Saint Paul writes, "God has also put his seal upon us and given the Spirit in our hearts as a first installment" (2 CORINTHIANS 1:21-22).

The Church teaches that those who die for the Faith can still be saved even without Baptism, as can catechumens—those who are preparing for Baptism. Similarly, those who haven't heard the Gospel, but, inspired by grace, sincerely desire God and seek to do His will, can also be saved without Baptism.

What about children who die before being baptized, as is the case with miscarriages or abortions? The Church invites us all to trust in the mercy of God and to pray for their salvation. Let us remember that God is love. If necessary, any person can baptize. (See our section on the Rite of Baptism, pages 20-21.)

To sum up, Baptism is a brand new beginning. It is a rebirth into a new life, a life in Christ Jesus, a supernatural life which begins in this world and continues forever in the next. We are new creations now, and it does not yet appear what we shall be, but we have God's promise that someday we too will live with Him in love, forever.

Beloved, we are God's children now; what we shall be has not yet been revealed. We do know that when it is revealed we shall be like him, for we shall see him as he is. Everyone who has this hope based on him makes himself pure, as he is pure.

1 John 3:2-3

And that's good news!

THE HISTORY OF BAPTISM

*Then Jesus came from Galilee to John at the Jordan
to be baptized by him.*
MATTHEW 3:13

When you think of water, what comes to mind? Water naturally reminds us of cleansing, of washing, of refreshing, and renewing. Water can bring life; it can also bring death.

The Exodus of the Jews through the Red Sea marked for them a sort of baptism, a passing over from slavery into sonship. Jews would also immerse themselves in baths to be cleansed of ritual impurity. In the waning days of the third decade AD, a fiery prophet named John appeared on the banks of the Jordan, preaching repentance from sins and offering a baptism of repentance to all who were ready and willing to turn from their sins and return to God.

Jesus came forward for John's baptism, though as the sinless Son of God, He did not need it for Himself. However, He did receive it, "to fulfill all righteousness" (MATTHEW 3:15). Jesus went down into the waters of the Jordan, and when He came up, the heavens were rent apart, and He saw the Spirit of God descending upon Him like a dove. At the same time, a voice from the heavens declared, "This is my beloved Son, with whom I am well pleased" (MATTHEW 3:16-17).

On the day of Pentecost, Peter and the apostles baptized 3,000 people, requiring them only to repent, accept Jesus as Messiah, and to be filled with His Holy Spirit. As time passed, the Church required a time of preparation and discernment for all who desired Baptism. Catechumens listened to the proclamation of God's Word, accepted the Gospel, and reformed their lives. This instruction period typically lasted one to three years. The Church would celebrate Baptism usually at the vigil of Easter, after the catechumens had spent time in focused prayer and fasting, preparing to receive their Bridegroom.

After the fall of the Roman Empire, the Church baptized infants much more readily and moved from Baptism by immersion to Baptism by pouring or sprinkling. By the time of the Council of Trent in the 16th century, the Church baptized infants and adults by having priests pour water over their heads while proclaiming, "I baptize you in the name of the Father, and of the Son, and of the Holy Spirit. Amen."

Today the Church typically baptizes infants within a month of their birth, often during a Sunday Mass. The Second Vatican Council renewed the ancient Rite of Christian Initiation of Adults (RCIA), a year-long preparation model from the early Church, in which adults (and children) prepare for their full initiation into the Body of Christ at the Easter Vigil through the sacraments of Baptism, Confirmation, and Holy Eucharist.

PREPARATION FOR BAPTISM

*"Let the children come to me, and do not prevent them;
for the kingdom of heaven belongs to such as these."*
MATTHEW 19:14

Since her early days, the Church has baptized infants, for
Baptism is a grace, an unearned gift from God. In such cases
the Church calls the parents and godparents of the newly
baptized to prepare themselves so that the child can better
receive and grow in God's wonderful grace.

As the primary teachers of the Faith for their children, parents
need to pass on their treasure of faith, and to ensure their
children receive their sacraments and attend Mass.

Godparents represent the Body of Christ—the Catholic
Church. They both assist in the preparation of candidates (or
their parents) and support them afterwards. Thus the Church
mandates that the godfather and godmother must be true
believers, who are able and indeed ready to help the newly
baptized godchildren to follow Christ their whole lives. Only
one godparent is necessary, while others can serve as witnesses.

Godparents must be at least 16 years old, baptized and also
confirmed—fully initiated Catholic Christians who are leading
a Christian life. Parents cannot be godparents as they already
have their own role in the faith life of their child.

If you are discerning whom to invite as godparent for yourself or your child, look for someone who has the faith to live out this calling, the time to develop a relationship with the newly baptized, and the willingness to get involved. Being a godparent is a vocation in its own right, so take your time.

Similarly, if someone has invited *you* to be a godparent, pray about your response. Are you willing to share your faith honestly and transparently? Do you live close enough to your potential godchild to get to know him or her? Are you an active parishioner? Most parishes require parents and godparents to attend a Baptism preparation class. It would be good to take this class with the parents to support them and ready yourself for your commitment. Finally, of course, you need to attend and participate in the Baptism itself.

Continue to pray for your godchild. At the appropriate age, give your godson or goddaughter a Bible, a book on the saints, and a prayer book, to help them get to know and fall in love with Jesus, His Father and their Holy Spirit, as well as Mary, Saint Joseph, and all the family! Every runner needs a good trainer, and good sponsors invest themselves in their godchildren.

Parents and godparents need to live in grace themselves, and to surround the child with grace, the abundance of God's life, which the child senses intuitively and spiritually and which affects the child in a very good and positive way. Remember, it takes a moment to be baptized, but a lifetime to be a saint!

THE RITE OF BAPTISM

Ordinarily, a bishop, priest, or deacon baptizes a person. In case of necessity, if no priest or deacon is available, anyone with the right intention can and should administer Baptism.

In the Rite of Baptism, the celebrant welcomes the family and sponsors, asking them what name they give their child and what they ask of God's Church. He instructs the parents that they have accepted the responsibility of raising their child in the Faith and training him or her to keep God's commandments, by loving God and neighbor. He asks them and the godparents for their commitment in this duty, and, in the name of the Christian community welcomes the child with joy and claims him or her for Christ our Savior by the sign of His Cross. The celebrant traces the cross on the child's forehead, and invites the parents and godparents to do the same.

After reading from Scripture, the celebrant preaches a homily and leads intercessory prayer. He invokes the Saints, and prays a prayer of exorcism over the power of Satan. He then anoints the child with sacred *chrism*, which is oil mixed with balsam that has been consecrated by the bishop, asking Christ to strengthen him with His power.

The celebrant blesses the Baptismal water, invoking the Holy Spirit, so that all who are buried with Christ in Baptism might rise also with Him to a new life. He then asks the parents and godparent to renew the vows of their own Baptism, to publicly reject Satan, his works, and his empty promises.

They reject sin and profess their faith in Christ Jesus and the Church by praying the Nicene Creed. The celebrant proclaims, "This is our faith. This is the faith of the Church. We are proud to profess it, in Christ Jesus our Lord." With the parents and godparents' approval, the celebrant baptizes the child in the name of the Father, and of the Son, and of the Holy Spirit.

He then anoints the child on the crown of the head with the chrism of salvation, praying that as Christ was anointed Priest, Prophet, and King, so may this newly baptized child live always as a member of His Body, sharing His everlasting life.

The celebrant then clothes the child in a white garment, signifying that he has become a new creation, and is clothed in Christ—praise God! The celebrant exhorts the child to see in this pure garment a sign of his Christian dignity, and prays that with the help of his family and friends the child will bring that dignity unstained into the everlasting life of heaven.

The celebrant gives the parents or godparents a lighted candle for the child, saying, "Receive the light of Christ." He exhorts them to keep the flame of faith burning brightly in the child, ending, "When the Lord comes, may he (she) go out to meet him with all the saints in the heavenly kingdom." Finally, he prays the *Ephphetha* or *Prayer Over Ears And Mouth*, asking Jesus to touch the child's ears and mouth to receive God's Word and proclaim his faith, to the praise and glory of God. All gathered pray the Lord's Prayer together. The celebrant then blesses the mother, father, and all present, and dismisses them.

THE EFFECTS AND FRUITS OF BAPTISM

We were indeed buried with him through baptism into death, so that, just as Christ was raised from the dead by the glory of the Father, we too might live in newness of life.

ROMANS 6:4

According to the *Catechism of the Catholic Church*, Baptism is the sacrament whereby Jesus, acting through the person who baptizes:

- cleanses us of Original Sin and any personal sins
- remits all punishment due to sin
- gives us new life by making us a new creation
- makes us adopted sons of the Father
- incorporates us into and makes us a member of Himself
- makes us a temple of the Holy Spirit
- makes us a member of His Body, the Church
- infuses us with sanctifying grace—"baptismal grace"
- imprints upon our soul an indelible spiritual sign, or character, which consecrates us for worship.

We become the temple of the Holy Spirit, and dwelling place of the Holy Trinity. "Do you not know that you are the temple of God, and that the Spirit of God dwells in you?" (1 CORINTHIANS 3:16). Where before we had only our own abilities, we now have the love of God flowing through us. We have His armor against the enemy, especially the sword of the Spirit— His Word.

To sum up, Baptism makes us pleasing and acceptable to God, for we receive the life of Jesus Himself into our spirits and souls. By God's gracious pleasure, we are given the grace to respond to His invitations, growing closer to Him through the Sacraments, especially the Holy Eucharist, and growing in love for one another. Baptism opens for us the gates of the kingdom of heaven, a foretaste and promise of the life we hope to share with God and His family forever.

That's a lot—and fittingly so. Let's face it; the sin of our first parents separated us from God and introduced death and evil into our human experience. We need a Savior who can not only rescue us from sin but also from its power over us, its grievous and clinging effects in our lives. Jesus has done this! His inestimable gift of Baptism floods us with the grace of a new life and the power to live that life in a manner worthy of our calling, to endure until the end, that, with our brothers and sisters in His Body, we might someday behold His face in glory!

So whoever is in Christ is a new creation: the old things have passed away; behold, new things have come.
2 CORINTHIANS 5:17

THE SACRAMENT OF CONFIRMATION

"But you will receive power when the holy Spirit comes upon you, and you will be my witnesses in Jerusalem ... to the ends of the earth."
ACTS 1:8

God chose a most amazing way to redeem us. He sent His Son to become flesh in the womb of the Virgin Mary. Thus, Jesus is both God and man. As God, Jesus was filled with divine power; as man He could bring this power to us. The Scriptures tell us that Jesus was filled with the Holy Spirit after His own baptism in the Jordan.

The Spirit led Jesus into the desert where He fasted and prayed forty days while He was tempted and tested by the devil. By obeying His Father and using His Word, Jesus overcame the temptations of the devil, and "returned to Galilee in the power of the Spirit, and news of him spread throughout the whole region" (LUKE 4:14)

Jesus went to Nazareth, where He had been raised, and entered the synagogue as He did every Sabbath. He stood up to read, and the attendant handed Him the scroll of Isaiah the prophet. Jesus unrolled the scroll and read the following passage from Isaiah Chapter 40:

> *"The Spirit of the Lord is upon me,*
> *because he has anointed me*
> *to bring glad tidings to the poor.*
> *He has sent me to proclaim liberty to captives*
> *and recovery of sight to the blind,*
> *to let the oppressed go free,*
> *and to proclaim a year acceptable to the Lord."*
> LUKE 4:18-19

He rolled up the scroll, handed it back to the attendant and sat down. Everyone in the synagogue fixed their eyes intently upon him. Then Jesus said, "Today this scripture passage is fulfilled in your hearing" (LUKE 4:20-21).

Jesus came to teach, heal, and liberate us by the power of His Holy Spirit, and to impart His Spirit to us so we could do the same for others! He won for us the gift of the Holy Spirit through His saving Passion, Death, and Resurrection, and poured out the Spirit upon the Church on Pentecost. The Spirit worked through the disciples as He had worked through Jesus, bringing liberation, joy, and healing to all believers who were made adopted children of their heavenly Father.

Although its path has not been as smooth, historically speaking, as some of the other sacraments, Confirmation is seen by the Church as the passing on of the gift of the Holy Spirit poured out on that first Pentecost. In other words, Confirmation is the sacramental spark that ignites the Spirit of Christ already present in our Baptism, completing the fullness of our initiation into Christ and His Body, and propelling us into witness for our faith by our words and deeds.

In Baptism, God made us His children; in Confirmation, He gives us a mission and the power to carry it out. Our primary mission is to *know* the Lord, with our minds and our hearts. When Martha complains that Mary isn't doing her share of serving, Jesus says, "Martha, Martha, you are anxious and worried about many things. There is need of only one thing. Mary has chosen the better part and it will not be taken from her" (LUKE 10:41-42).

What is "the better part" that Mary chose? Was it not to receive God's love flowing into her heart? Was it not to receive God's Word streaming into her ears? Here then is the counsel of Jesus for all His followers: "Get to know Me first. Spend time with Me. You need Me more than others need you." If we fulfill this primary mission, God will equip us to carry out the rest of His Will, and fulfill our mission. We can't; God can; so let Him!

The Holy Spirit thus anoints us with the experiential knowledge that we are deeply and unconditionally loved. He then calls us to be witnesses of this new life of faith. He strengthens us to fight sin and gives us His gifts, as Saint Paul says, "for the common good" (1 CORINTHIANS 12:7 RSV, CATHOLIC EDITION). The Holy Spirit poured out sacramentally in Confirmation calls us to share our gifts with others.

We can see why Confirmation was originally received immediately after Baptism. It is clear that Confirmation is actually just the beginning of our Christian life, just as Jesus began His ministry only after He had been anointed with the Spirit and with power after His baptism.

Confirmation, like Baptism, imparts a special character, or seal, on those who are confirmed, and hence it cannot be repeated. The minister of Confirmation imposes or lays his hands on the candidates and anoints them with chrism, saying, "Be sealed with the Gift of the Holy Spirit."

The reception of the sacrament of Confirmation is necessary for the completion of baptismal grace. For "by the sacrament of Confirmation, [the baptized] are more perfectly bound to the Church and are enriched with a special strength of the Holy Spirit. Hence they are, as true witnesses of Christ, more strictly obliged to spread and defend the faith by word and deed" (CCC 1285).

THE HISTORY OF CONFIRMATION

For the first few centuries after Pentecost, Confirmation was considered more a part of Baptism than a separate sacrament. Catechumens were immersed in the baptismal water and anointed with oil, to receive the fullness of the Spirit of Christ. Usually it was the bishop who anointed these newly baptized and laid his hands on their heads for an outpouring of the Holy Spirit. Each new Catholic would then join the rest of the community for the first time at the Eucharist.

Even so, baptismal liturgies varied throughout the young and rapidly growing Church. There was no set way the sacraments were administered. Early Christians developed their theology as they moved along with the Spirit of God which was working mightily in and around them, freeing the world of its darkness and bringing the light of Christ.

With the acceptance of Christianity in 4th-century Rome, the great number of converts made it impossible for the bishop to anoint each one at their Baptism. In the Eastern Empire, the bishop would bless oil—*myron*—and the priest would use it to anoint the newly baptized, signifying the bishop's presence and acceptance of them into the Christian community. In the Western Empire, the Church provided a separate ceremony for the bishop to personally anoint the new Christian with chrism, "confirming" their Baptism. Because of the difficulty in traveling, over time these episcopal visits grew further apart, and Confirmation fell pretty much into disuse.

By the end of the first millennium, the faithful were again seeking the sacrament of Confirmation. The Council of Trent in the mid-16th century affirmed that Confirmation was one of the seven sacraments of the Church; it strengthened the faith of the believers and fortified them against temptation. The bishop was the ordinary minister of Confirmation, but he could delegate a priest to administer it.

Today, some bishops are returning Confirmation to its original position after Baptism and before Eucharist. In their dioceses, children are confirmed around the age of 7-9, prior to their First Communion. In other dioceses, Catholics are confirmed as teens, after a period of spiritual and catechetical formation. Candidates choose the name of a saint as their Confirmation name, and the sacrament is usually celebrated within Mass.

It is a great blessing to know Jesus as our Savior. The Holy Spirit gives us the power to discover and proclaim Him as Lord. In fact, Saint Paul says that "no one can say, 'Jesus is Lord,' except by the holy Spirit" (1 CORINTHIANS 12:3). The Holy Spirit wants us to surrender ourselves to the Lordship of Jesus, to give Him permission to complete His creation in us, that we might become fully human and fully holy. We cannot do this by ourselves, but only through the power given us from on high, through the sevenfold gift of the Holy Spirit. Thus let us pray constantly, "Veni, Sancte Spiritus—Come, Holy Spirit!"

PREPARATION FOR CONFIRMATION

The next day John was there again with two of his disciples,
and as he watched Jesus walk by, he said, "Behold, the Lamb of
God." The two disciples heard what he said and followed Jesus.
Jesus turned and saw them following him and said to them,
"What are you looking for?" They said to him, "Rabbi"
(which translated means Teacher), "where are you staying?"
He said to them, "Come, and you will see." So they went
and saw where he was staying, and they stayed with him that day.
JOHN 1:35-39

When we consider how to best prepare for an encounter with the Holy Spirit, it seems wise to imitate the first disciples. They didn't *do* anything, at first. They simply went to stay with Jesus. They didn't preach, or heal, or testify. All they did was stay with Jesus. Like Mary, the sister of Lazarus, they simply remained, in a sense, at His feet, listening to Him, eating with Him, getting to know Him. Years later, observing the apostles' boldness in their defense of the miraculous cure of a lame man, the members of the Sanhedrin "were astonished, and they took note that these men had been with Jesus" (ACTS 4:13-NIV).

The best way, then, to prepare for the coming of the Holy Spirit is to spend time with Jesus, to rest in His presence. It is good to surrender your day to Him upon awakening, to invite Him into your heart again each day. It is good to celebrate the Eucharist and to receive Jesus in this most intimate and Holy Communion. A popular way of abiding in Christ is to visit Him in the Blessed Sacrament or especially in Eucharistic Adoration where that is available.

The next step is to read the Scriptures, and especially Jesus' words, which "are spirit and life" (JOHN 6:63). God's Word has the power to transform us on the inside, to heal us and to prepare us for a greater endowment of His love and grace. It also instructs us on the truths of our new life in Christ, and counsels us how to grow in faith, hope, and charity.

Another part of your preparation is to choose a Confirmation sponsor. Your sponsor is someone who will help to guide, encourage, and mentor you in your faith. A sponsor must be a confirmed Catholic, at least 16 years old, and a practicing member of the Church, who is not your parent.

When discerning whom to choose as your sponsor, look for someone who loves Jesus, who is authentically trying to live their faith. Look for a prayerful man or woman who is willing to spend some time with you. A sponsor cares for you and listens to you, as you both continue your journey of faith.

We encourage you to go the Sacrament of Reconciliation and make a good Confession. In the sacrament of Penance we are reconciled with God and the Church, the eternal punishment incurred by mortal sins is remitted, and some or all of the temporal punishment of sin is removed. In addition, we regain a serenely peaceful conscience and an increase of spiritual fortitude to help us fight the good fight.

May God bless you and fill you with His Holy Spirit!

THE RITE OF CONFIRMATION

The essential rite of Confirmation includes the anointing with oil and the laying on of hands. The bishop, or his representative, uses sacred chrism for the anointing, which, as explained earlier, is consecrated oil mixed with balsam.

The Sacrament of Confirmation is usually celebrated during Mass. The candidates typically sit together with their sponsors, reminiscent of Mary and the disciples, who gathered in the upper room after Jesus' Ascension, praying together as they awaited the gift of the Holy Spirit.

After the Gospel, the pastor (or another priest, deacon, or catechist) presents the candidates for Confirmation to the bishop, who then gives a brief homily, explaining the Scripture readings and giving everyone present a deeper understanding of the gift of the Holy Spirit given in Confirmation.

After the homily, the bishop asks the candidates to renew their Baptismal promises and to profess their faith, the faith of the Church. In this renewal, the candidates publicly reject Satan and accept for themselves the faith of their Baptism, thus announcing their intention to be fully initiated into their Catholic faith.

The laying on of hands expresses the biblical gesture of calling down the gift and gifts of the Holy Spirit. The bishop extends his hands over the candidates and prays for God to send His Holy Spirit upon them as their Advocate, to help and guide them. He prays for God to give them the spirit of wisdom and understanding, of right judgment and courage, of knowledge and true reverence. He asks God to fill them with the spirit of wonder and awe in His unimaginable presence.

Each candidate walks up to the bishop. The candidate's sponsor places his right hand on the latter's shoulder and gives the candidate's name to the bishop; the bishop dips his right thumb in the chrism and makes the Sign of the Cross on the forehead of the one to be confirmed, as he says: "Be sealed with the Gift of the Holy Spirit." Through this anointing, each candidate receives in his or her soul the indelible character, or seal, of the Holy Spirit, along with the grace of the Holy Spirit conforming him or her more closely to Christ Jesus. The newly confirmed responds with a heartfelt "Amen!"

The bishop then shares the sign of peace with the newly confirmed, and Holy Mass proceeds as usual.

THE EFFECTS AND FRUITS OF CONFIRMATION

As the bishop anoints the candidate, God pours out on him or her the gift of the Holy Spirit, like that received on the first Pentecost. Confirmation imprints an indelible spiritual mark, or character, on our soul, signifying that Jesus has sealed us with His Spirit. It roots us more deeply in divine sonship and unites us more closely to Christ. Confirmation renews and invigorates the gifts of the Holy Spirit (such as those listed in ISAIAH 11:2-3 and 1 CORINTHIANS 12:7-11) in our soul, and gives us a special power to witness to our faith publicly.

Here is how the *Catechism of the Catholic Church* states it:

"From this fact, Confirmation brings an increase and deepening of baptismal grace:

- it roots us more deeply in the divine filiation which makes us cry, 'Abba! Father!';
- it unites us more firmly to Christ;
- it increases the gifts of the Holy Spirit in us;
- it renders our bond with the Church more perfect;
- it gives us a special strength of the Holy Spirit to spread and defend the faith by word and action as true witnesses of Christ, to confess the name of Christ boldly, and never to be ashamed of the Cross:

Recall then that you have received the spiritual seal, the spirit of wisdom and understanding, the spirit of right judgment and courage, the spirit of knowledge and reverence, the spirit of holy fear in God's presence. Guard what you have received. God the Father has marked you with his sign; Christ the Lord has confirmed you and has placed his pledge, the Spirit, in your hearts.

(SAINT AMBROSE, DE MYSTERIIS)

"Like Baptism which it completes, Confirmation is given only once, for it too imprints on the soul an *indelible spiritual mark*, the 'character,' which is the sign that Jesus Christ has marked a Christian with the seal of His Spirit by clothing him with power from on high so that he may be His witness.

"This 'character' perfects the common priesthood of the faithful, received in Baptism, and 'the confirmed person receives the power to profess faith in Christ publicly and as it were officially'" (CCC 1303-1305).

In the sacrament of Confirmation, Jesus fills *you* with the same Spirit that came upon Mary and the disciples at that first Pentecost. Jesus calls you first of all to Himself, that you would find in Him a true Friend, who knows your hopes and dreams, your struggles and successes. Jesus wants you to feel His personal love for *you*, and then to share this love with others. Jesus died, rose, and sent His Spirit so all people could receive His salvation, live a fully human and holy life, and enjoy eternal life with the Blessed Trinity in heaven. And that's Good News!

THE GIFT OF THE HOLY EUCHARIST

God's passionate desire to bring all humanity into an eternal communion with Himself remains the same yesterday, today, and forever. After the Fall of our first parents, God made a covenant with Abraham, through whom He would form a people, and send His promised Redeemer.

In the Passover, God commanded each Hebrew family to sacrifice an unblemished male lamb and to apply its blood on the doorposts and lintel of each house. He commanded them to eat its flesh roasted, with unleavened bread. The blood of the Passover lamb marked the houses of the Israelites; and God delivered them from Egypt. The Lord commanded the Jews to keep the Passover as a memorial feast throughout their generations, of how He had freed Israel from bondage and established a covenant with them, that they might be His people, and that He might be their God.

On the night before He died, Jesus gathered His twelve apostles, and together they came to the upper room to celebrate the Passover. During the meal, Jesus took the bread, gave thanks, blessed it, and said, "This is my body, which will be given for you; do this in memory of me" (LUKE 22:19).

Jesus then took the large chalice of wine, blessed it, and gave it to His disciples, saying, "Drink from it, all of you, for this is my blood of the covenant, which will be shed on behalf of many for the forgiveness of sins" (MATTHEW 26:27-28).

Jesus thus instituted a new and eternal covenant by changing the Passover bread and wine into His own Body and Blood. The Church calls this mystery the Transubstantiation. He who would be sacrificed on Calvary shared the covenant meal with His apostles, ushering in a *New* Covenant with all of us, Jew and Gentile alike. Jesus invited His apostles to enter into a true communion—a sacramental union—with Himself. He commissioned and commanded them to continue celebrating this Eucharist, so named from the Greek word *Eucharistia*—Thanksgiving. It was the first Mass: the Holy Sacrifice and the Sacred Meal.

On Good Friday, laden with the sins of the whole world, Jesus died for us in obedience to His Father and in accordance with the Scriptures. "For our sake he made him to be sin who did not know sin, so that we might become the righteousness of God in him" (2 CORINTHIANS 5:21). Son of God and Son of Man, the humble and obedient Lamb of God offered Himself completely to His Father. God accepted the sacrifice of His Son. The atonement was completed, and satisfaction was made.

In the Eucharist, Jesus makes present again His sacrificial offering of Himself to His Father at Calvary, and His giving of Himself as sacred food so all can commune with Him. This inestimable gift makes present Christ's death and Resurrection.

Jesus' greatest gift to us was the gift of Himself, in the Holy Eucharist. The Holy Eucharist is the Body and Blood of Jesus Christ, present under the appearance of bread and wine. Jesus gave us Himself as food for our souls, because of His great love for each of us, because He wanted to be always with us, and He wanted us to have abundant life in Him.

Jesus told His apostles, "Do this in memory of me." He wanted them to continue giving the gift of His Body and Blood to everyone who believed in Him. As a Good Shepherd, Jesus wanted to ensure that His sheep would be fed down through the centuries, which His Church has done, to this very day.

When we receive Jesus in the Eucharist, He promises that we will be strengthened with Him in this life and remain with Him forever in the next. Jesus said, "I am the bread of life; whoever comes to me will never hunger, and whoever believes in me will never thirst" (JOHN 6:35).

The Eucharist makes us one with Jesus, our Good Shepherd. The Eucharist also unites us to one another, as members of His Body. Jesus' Body and Blood gives us true life, and helps us to love God, all people, and ourselves as well.

THE HISTORY OF THE MASS

By 150 AD, the basic structure of the Eucharist was in place.
Saint Justin Martyr tells us that Mass was celebrated on
Sundays, that it was "the Flesh and Blood of Jesus Incarnate,"
to which the community gave their assent with their "Amen."
There were two readings, a homily and a procession of gifts, a
collection for the poor, the Eucharistic Prayer, and the giving
of Communion.

As Christianity came to be accepted in the empire,
Constantine built basilicas—large churches modeled on the
Roman public halls—for the Christians to use. Saint Ambrose
of Milan and others composed hymns such as the magnificent
hymn, *Te Deum*, so everyone could honor God together. The
worshippers sang the Gloria, Sanctus, and the Agnus Dei.

With the introduction of basilicas, bishops, priests, and
deacons wore more formal clothing, handed down to us as the
vestments of the Mass. The readings of the Mass were taken
from the Old and New Testaments. The celebrant "broke
open" the Word in his homily, so Christ could be received
both at the table of the Word and in His presence *par excellence*
at the table of the Eucharist. All of this was focused on one
overarching theme: The Body of Christ in the Eucharist—*corpus
mysticum*, according to the Fathers of the Church—makes the
Body of Christ—*corpus verum*—which is the Church. The
Eucharist is given to transform *us* into the Body of Christ!

In 1545, Pope Paul III convened the Council of Trent to clarify Catholic doctrine on salvation, sacraments, Scripture, and Tradition. The Council standardized the Mass, decreeing a uniformity followed by the Church for centuries. In 1570, Pope Saint Pius V produced the Roman Missal—the standard for the Roman Rite.

The priest would be the celebrant, the acolytes would represent the community, and the people would participate more interiorly in the Holy Sacrifice of the Mass. Everything, including the readings, was read in Latin. The Council of Trent restated the eternal truths of the liturgy, and gave to the faithful an ordered, true presentation of the Mass.

Since the liturgy is alive, after four centuries the Church needed the Holy Spirit to breathe upon her children, renewing their faith and helping them celebrate the Eucharist in new and life-giving ways, while not discarding the beauty and reverence of the old.

The seeds of the liturgical renewal sprouted in the mid-19th century, with the revival of Gregorian chant and studies of liturgical history. In 1909, an international conference on the liturgy stressed the need for the active participation of the laity. Father Romano Guardini and others urged Catholics to see beyond the externals of the liturgy, beautiful as they were, to encounter the Lord waiting to meet us. Pope Pius XII called for the community to have the true spirit of the liturgy, to realize and reverence the Real Presence of Christ in the Eucharist.

In the pivotal document *Sacrosanctum Concilium*—The Constitution on the Sacred Liturgy—issued in 1963, the Vatican II Council Fathers emphasized that the Eucharist is the source and summit of our lives. They called all worshippers to a full, conscious, and active participation, "which is demanded by the very nature of the liturgy." We gain our "true Christian spirit" primarily and indispensably from the sacred liturgy, "and therefore pastors of souls must zealously strive to achieve it."

The Mass of Pope Paul VI became the ordinary or normal form of the Roman Rite Mass. This Mass retained the essential structure of the Tridentine Mass, while eliminating elements such as the prayers at the foot of the altar, the silent praying of the Canon, and the reading of John 1:1-14—the Last Gospel— at the end of Mass. Mass was now offered in the vernacular, the treasury of Sacred Scripture was opened more fully, and the faithful were invited to participate more fully in the liturgy.

Pope Benedict XVI, as a seminarian, studied Father Guardini's seminal work, *The Spirit of the Liturgy*. He wrote that Guardini's book "helped us to rediscover the liturgy in all its beauty, hidden wealth, and time-transcending grandeur...." It motivated him, and others, to seek for a more "substantial" celebration of the liturgy as the prayer of the Church, inspired and directed by the Holy Spirit Himself, "a prayer in which Christ unceasingly becomes contemporary with us, and enters into our lives."

After his election as pope in 2005, the Holy Father issued the Motu Proprio—"on his own initiative"—*Summorum Pontificum*, liberalizing the use of the 1962 Roman Missal. He reiterated that the ordinary liturgy of the Roman Church was the one promulgated by Pope Paul VI, commonly used today. He stated, however, that the Roman Missal—the Tridentine Mass—promulgated by Pope Saint Pius V and re-issued by Blessed Pope John XXIII, is to be considered an extraordinary expression of the liturgy, and therefore he extended his permission for all priests to celebrate that traditional Latin Mass. Priests could use either Missal without needing permission from the local bishop, and were also allowed to administer the other sacraments in their pre-Vatican II format.

Pope Benedict wanted to help Traditionalist Catholics reconcile "in the heart of the Church." He also wanted other Catholics to have an opportunity to experience the Latin Mass, through which, for centuries, the Lord has nourished the spiritual life of many saints, built up His presence in many people, and "fecundated (enriched) their piety."

PREPARATION FOR HOLY COMMUNION

God prepared Israel for thousands of years to receive the Messiah. When the time drew near, God sent John the Baptist to prepare His way. Jesus Himself sent His disciples out ahead of Him to prepare the people for His arrival.

Is it not true that the greater the event, the more time it takes to get ready for it? God's gift of His only-begotten Son to us as our Messiah is the most precious and priceless gift imaginable. In truth, we really can't fully understand it because it is a great mystery. Thus God prepared Israel, and specifically the people of Jesus' time, for the Messiah, so they would be as ready as possible to hear Him, receive His words, and follow Him when He finally came!

Jesus chose to give Himself to us in the Holy Eucharist so we could receive Him as our spiritual food and always have His presence in our hearts, Therefore, we need to prepare ourselves the best we can to receive our dear Lord.

First of all, we need to examine our conscience and ask forgiveness for any ways we have turned from God or injured ourselves or others. If we have serious sin, we need to receive the Sacrament of Reconciliation.

We need to fast from food and drink (except water) for one hour before going to Holy Communion. This fast was originally from midnight until Mass the next day, but was later modified to a three-hour fast and finally to one hour. We fast in this way to prepare ourselves physically to receive the Bread of Life.

Similarly, it is good to prepare ourselves spiritually to receive God's Word, which is spirit and life. A time-honored method of preparation is to read the Gospel and the Readings before Mass and take some time reflecting on them. What is the Lord saying to you, to His Body, and to all humanity, through the Readings of the day?

When you get to church, take time before Mass to be quiet and enter the presence of the Lord. Speak to Our Lord; tell Him you believe Him, hope in Him, and love Him. During Mass, sing the hymns, listen to the readings, and pray the prayers with all your heart. Ask our Blessed Mother Mary to make you ready to receive her Son. When you go up to Communion, tell Jesus, "I greatly desire to receive You, dear Jesus!"

Finally, when you do receive Jesus, let Him do the talking; listen to Him; let Him just love you. The rest will follow, if we will only abide in Him!

THE BENEFITS OF HOLY COMMUNION

Koinonia is the Greek word first used to describe communion. Koinonia means a family bond, a union, a sense of comforting love that we share. When we receive Holy Communion, we receive Jesus Christ, Body and Blood, Soul and Divinity. In Christ we experience again our essential union shared with all who are members of His Body. We commune with the Head and the members. In one sense, it could be said that we also receive one another in Holy Communion.

The *Catechism of the Catholic Church* in paragraphs 1391-1398 lists the following fruits—benefits—of Holy Communion:

- **Holy Communion increases our union with the Lord.** Remember Jesus' parable about the vine and the branches? A dead branch withers and dies apart from the vine. In like manner we need the Eucharist to keep us strong in Christ.

- **Holy Communion nourishes our spirits with all we need to grow spiritually.** It often imparts physical strength as well!

- **Holy Communion separates us from sin and its power.**

- **Holy Communion strengthens God's love within us.** It revives our hearts and empowers us to root ourselves in Christ.

- **Holy Communion preserves us from falling into mortal sin.** The closer we are to Christ, the harder it is for the enemy to pull us away from Him.

- **Holy Communion deepens our unity as Church.** The Eucharist actually makes the Church! Communion deepens our unity as the Body of Christ.
- **Holy Communion constrains us to recognize Christ in the poor and invites us to serve them.**
- **Holy Communion causes us to long for the full unity of all Christians and invites us to pray "that they may all be one"** (JOHN 17:21).

After Communion, the priest invites us to pray silently, and then he prays the Prayer after Communion, thanking God for the incredible gift of the Eucharist we have received. Amen!

The priest then gives us his final blessing.

God promised Abraham that all the earth would find blessing in him (GENESIS 12:3). To bless someone is wish them well, to speak good to them, or to give them a good. All blessings flow from God, the creator of heaven and earth. By virtue of their ordination, a bishop, priest, or deacon conveys by his blessing the Church's sacramental power.

Let us seek to receive the final blessing with a fervent confidence and joy, for God's powerful blessing shields us from our spiritual enemies and brings His protection, especially at our death. Pope Benedict XVI has said that God wants only love and life, for all people and at all times. We are blessed to be a blessing, to the whole world!

THE SACRAMENTS OF HEALING

God created a beautiful world, and a human family with whom He could share Himself and His heaven. But then the unimaginable happened. Our first parents failed the test God allowed them to experience. And with the Fall came the consequences of sin—separation, woundedness, sickness, and death.

The Gospels clearly teach that Jesus came to set us free, and to heal us in spirit, soul, and body. His very name, *Yeshua*, means *God shall save*, and indeed Jesus came to deliver us from our bondage to sin and heal us of its spiritual, physical, mental, and social effects.

Many of us view our spiritual and physical ills as serious, if not hopeless, problems. But God isn't like us. He sees all that has gone wrong with the world as an opportunity for Him to demonstrate His unconditional and unfailing love for each of us. Jesus was born with a mission, ordained by His Father, to suffer and die for us in order that we might be liberated from sin and all its consequences, including death itself.

The Sacraments of Initiation bring us into Christ and His new life, but we all need healing as we continue our walk in the Lord. Jesus provides this healing for us in our spirits, souls, and bodies through the sacraments of Penance and the Anointing of the Sick.

THE SACRAMENT OF PENANCE

Jesus said to them again, "Peace be with you. ...
Receive the holy Spirit.
Whose sins you forgive are forgiven them,
and whose sins you retain are retained."

JOHN 20:21; 22-23

Peace be with you!
Why did Jesus choose
these as His very first
words to His Apostles
after His passion, death
and resurrection? Could
it be that this is our
most basic human need
of all—peace of mind,

peace of soul, peace of heart? **Peace:** safety from anxiety, from
oppression, from assault. **Peace:** inner serenity, inner
happiness, inner joy. **Peace:** to be home with Jesus in your
heart. This is the peace—*shalom*—He came to give us, the peace
Jesus won for us at the cost of His own life.

Because of his affliction
he shall see the light in fullness of days;
Through his suffering, my servant shall justify many,
and their guilt he shall bear.

ISAIAH 53:11

God loves you! He created you because He deeply desires to live with you forever. God reaches out to us first and offers us the free gift of His grace, as we have seen, in the precious sacrament of Baptism.

As wonderful as Baptism is, we can weaken and even lose God's life within us by sin, which wounds God, our fellow believers, and ourselves. There is no evil graver than sin, which harms so many.

Thankfully, Jesus has given His Church the remedy for this universal sickness. In the sacrament of Penance, also called Reconciliation or Confession, God forgives our sins.

Penance itself as a name for this sacrament comes from *paenitentia*, the Latin word meaning penitence or repentance. Initially this word meant the same as *metanoia*, the Greek word for an inner change of heart, or conversion. Later *paenitentia* came to represent outer practices of repentance, today called penance. Over the centuries, this sacrament has retained three essential elements: repentance and contrition on the part of the believer, confession of sin, and forgiveness, mediated through the absolution of the priest.

The Church Fathers speak of two conversions: the waters of Baptism and the tears of repentance. Through the sacrament of Penance, which consists of repentance, confession of sins, and reparation, God, who is rich in mercy, restores us to communion with Himself. Christ, through the priest, absolves us of all sin.

Perfect contrition is repentance arising from a deep love of God; imperfect contrition arises from other motives. We must confess to a priest all the unconfessed grave sins we remember. He then proposes a penance to help us repair sin's harm.

In the sacrament of Penance we are reconciled with God and the Church, the eternal punishment incurred by mortal sins is remitted, and some or all of the temporal punishment of sin is removed. In addition, we regain a serenely peaceful conscience and an increase of spiritual fortitude to help us fight the good fight.

Pope John Paul II urged the use of traditional forms of the sacrament of Penance but urged a renewed inner sense of the Holy Spirit. The form of the structure is always meant to lead us to the freedom of the Spirit.

> *Now the Lord is the Spirit, and where the Spirit*
> *of the Lord is, there is freedom.*
> 2 CORINTHIANS 3:17

THE HISTORY OF PENANCE

God was reconciling the world to himself in Christ,
not counting their trespasses against them
and entrusting to us the message of reconciliation.
2 CORINTHIANS 5:19

Jesus' very nature was—and is—forgiving. God was reconciling
us to Himself in Christ, forgiving us even before we asked for
it. Knowing we would need forgiveness even after receiving
Baptism, Jesus passed on this power to His apostles in His very
first visit to them after His Resurrection (CF. JOHN 20:23).

In the early Church, those who committed serious sins such as
murder, idolatry, or adultery, were barred from the community
until they repented publicly and turned away from death back
to life in Christ. In the next century, this practice became
more ritualized, and a penitent could undergo it only once.

Meanwhile, in Ireland and the British Isles, monks were
dealing with the ever present problem of human weakness in a
different and more creative manner. A novice would be
assigned an older monk as his mentor or "sponsor." The two
would gather weekly to share how their lives were going, and
the younger monk would confess his weaknesses and sins to
the older. They would end by praying together for forgiveness
and healing.

As the Irish monks, and others, ministered to the Germanic
tribes who were converting large-scale to the faith, they shared
this practice as a way to help the new Christians remain alive
and vibrant in their faith.

In time, this practice of Confession spread through the whole Church, as people confessed their sins to priests, received a penance, and then received absolution.

Initially the penance matched the offense. For instance, fighting and bloodshed might incur a scourging and prohibition from carrying weapons. Later, confessors began giving the praying of prayers as a penance—for instance, praying part or all of the Rosary, or perhaps some of the Psalms.

Initially, a penitent was absolved only after he or she had performed the required penance. However, over time, due to a variety of factors, priests first absolved penitents and then assigned a required penance to be carried out after the Confession itself.

All sin is an offense against God, and sin came to be classified as either mortal—seriously sinful, even to the death of grace in the soul—or venial, which was less sinful, so that God's life and grace remained in the soul, although His grace was lessened.

Then there was the distinction between perfect and imperfect contrition. Perfect contrition is sorrow for sin because we have hurt God whom we love. This contrition produces a firm resolve of amendment and a true conversion in the life and actions of the penitent. Imperfect contrition is sorrow motivated by fear of punishment and the consequences of sin. This type of contrition does not necessarily have the power to move someone to *metanoia*, true repentance and conversion.

Saint Thomas Aquinas defined the sacrament of Penance as both the sorrow and contrition of the penitent, which they evidenced by their acts of penance, and the absolution spoken by the priest in the sacrament. He saw this sacrament as a real help in our calling to be holy, to be what God made us in our Baptism:

> But you are "a chosen race, a royal priesthood, a holy nation, a people of his own, so that you may announce the praise" of him who called you out of darkness into his wonderful light.
> 1 PETER 2:9

Pope John Paul II repeatedly called us to "be who you are"—to be holy, to allow Christ Jesus to live vibrantly in us! Saint Thomas Aquinas believed that as we cooperate with the grace of Penance and the other sacraments, we can in fact become morally good; we can eventually replace our sinful habits and tendencies with good habits of virtue.

Even so, abuses crept into the sacrament of Penance, perhaps most notably the buying and selling of indulgences. Martin Luther and other Protestant reformers "protested" such practices, with some good reason, but unfortunately went too far and ultimately dismissed the sacrament.

In response, the Council of Trent reiterated the belief that Jesus wanted us to confess our sins, especially our serious sins, to receive forgiveness, grace, and peace. The Council took a somewhat legalistic stance and set the mold for the sacrament of Penance for the next 400 years.

Vatican II and scriptural research renewed the idea that our connection with God was based not on law but on covenant—His covenant with Israel and His New Covenant with us given by Jesus at the Last Supper. Thus sin is not just a breaking away, but really is more a breaking of a relationship, turning away from the One who loves us, to pursue our own will. Vatican II also fashioned new forms of the Rite of Penance.

Most common today are either one of these:

1. **Private form of the Sacrament of Reconciliation:**
   - In addition to being separated by a screen, the priest and penitent have the option of facing one another where the Confessional allows this.
   - The priest implores God's mercy before giving absolution.
   - The priest has the option of giving other penances besides the praying of prayers.

2. **A Communal penance service:**
   - A Prayer Service including worship hymns and Scripture readings.
   - All confess privately to a priest and receive absolution.

The most popular age for First Reconciliation remains around 7 years of age—the age of discretion, also called the age of reason. Today, beyond minimal confession of sin, more people are seeking spiritual direction for guidance as to how they can more completely seek God and discern His Will.

PREPARATION FOR PENANCE

Jesus loves you! He created you to live with Him forever. He calls you to love God with all your heart, soul, mind, and strength, and to love others as yourself. Sometimes we turn away from Jesus. This sin separates us from God. But Jesus, who died for us, loves us too much to let us remain apart. He wants very much to forgive us if only we repent. This we do through the Sacrament of Reconciliation.

EXAMINATION OF CONSCIENCE

The Ten Commandments

1. **I am the Lord, Your God. You shall have no other gods before Me.**
   Do I pray every day? Do I worship God alone? Have I participated in any superstitious practices? Do I let the things of this world (internet, entertainment, money, etc.) take precedence over love of God?

2. **You shall not take the name of the Lord in vain.**
   Do I respect God's name? Do I misuse it out of frustration or anger or to impress those around me? Am I willing to stand up for God, to speak of Him to others?

3. **Remember to keep holy the Lord's day.**
   Do I attend Mass on Sundays and Holy Days? Do I participate by praying and singing? Do I listen closely to the Scripture readings? Do I refrain from work on Sundays except when necessary, and spend time with my family?

4. **Honor your Father and Mother.**

   God puts people in authority to care for us, protect us, and guide us. Do I obey my parents/superiors willingly? Do I help out at home? Do I respect older people?

5. **You shall not kill.**

   Do I taunt or fight with others? Have I abused my body with alcohol or other drugs? Do I forgive readily or do I seek revenge?

6. **You shall not commit adultery.**

   When two people get married, they promise their mutual love to one other. God wants them to honor that promise, and He wants all of us to be pure and modest in our behavior. Do I treat my body with respect? Have I kept myself pure in thought, word, and deed?

7. **You shall not steal.**

   Am I trustworthy and faithful to my word? Do I respect other people's property? Have I stolen or damaged what belongs to another? Have I been honest in my work?

8. **You shall not lie.**

   Have I lied to protect myself or 'get away' with something? Have I gossiped about others or damaged their reputation in any way?

9. **You shall not covet your neighbor's wife.**

   Marriage is a great blessing, a very special gift from God. If married, have I weakened or damaged my marriage by desiring another person? Do I spend time with my spouse? Do I help others remains faithful to their commitments?

10. **You shall not covet your neighbor's goods.**

    Am I jealous or envious of the things that others have? Am I grateful for all God has given me? Do I share with others?

THE RITE OF PENANCE

PRAYER BEFORE CONFESSION

Dear Father, I come before You today and admit that I have sinned against heaven and against You. I repent of my sins. Create in me a clean heart, O God, and renew a steadfast spirit within me. I want to live in freedom and joy—to be fully alive, made whole by Your grace and forgiveness. Grant me the honesty to know my sins, the humility to confess them, and the grace to avoid them. Dear Mother Mary, please help me make a good Confession and be filled with the peace of Christ. Amen.

HOW TO GO TO CONFESSION

- Make the Sign of the Cross: **"Bless me Father, for I have sinned. It has been _____ since my last Confession."**
- Confess your sins.
- When you have finished, say, **"I am sorry for these and all my sins."**
- The priest will give you a penance, and he may offer you some spiritual direction.
- Pray an Act of Contrition.

ACT OF CONTRITION

O my God, I am heartily sorry for having offended You. I detest all my sins because of Your just punishments, but most of all because they offend You, my God, who are all good and deserving of all my love. I firmly resolve, with the help of Your grace, to sin no more and to avoid the near occasions of sin. Amen.

PRAYER AFTER CONFESSION

Dear God, thank You so much for forgiving me! I feel lighter, forgiven, renewed, and ready to go on with my life. I want to walk in freedom from sin, and to avoid the occasions and places that would lead me back into it. Lord, I admit I can't do it without You, so please, through the intercession of Our Blessed Mother Mary, of Saint Joseph, her most chaste spouse, and of all the Saints, help me to continue living in peace and joy with You and others. In Jesus' name. Amen.

THE FRUITS AND EFFECTS OF PENANCE

Jesus' gift of Faith to all believers is more than a religion; it's a relationship! Jesus came to *restore* our union with His Father, to reconcile us to God. He also came to restore us to union with one another, and finally to a union with our true selves. He came to seek and save what was lost.

The Church teaches that the effects of the sacrament of Penance are:

- **Reconciliation with God.** We recover grace, the life of God in our soul.
- **Reconciliation with the Church.** We are reunited spiritually with our brothers and sisters in the Body of Christ.
- **The eternal punishment incurred by serious mortal sin is remitted.**
- **The temporal punishment resulting from sin is remitted, at least in part.**
- God gives us peace and serenity, a clear conscience, and spiritual consolation.
- God gives us an increase of spiritual inner strength to continue to battle sin and live in virtue.

The Sacrament of Reconciliation, Penance, or Confession, is yet another opportunity to experience God's love. "For the LORD is good; his mercy endures forever" (JEREMIAH 33:11).

THE PRECEPTS OF THE CHURCH

I urge you... by the mercies of God, to offer your bodies as a living sacrifice, holy and pleasing to God, your spiritual worship.
ROMANS 12:1

We are saved and justified by God's free gift of grace and our willing response. We fulfill our calling *in* the Church, in union with our baptized brothers and sisters. From the Church we receive God's Word: *the law of Christ*, and His grace in the sacraments: *the way of Christ*. Mary is our model and helper in following Christ who is the Way, the Truth, and the Life.

The Catechism of the Catholic Church lists the following precepts as obligatory laws—the minimum necessary to offer God our spiritual worship, growing in love for Him and our neighbor.

- To attend Mass on Sundays and holy days of obligation, and rest from servile labor.
- To confess our sins at least once a year.
- To receive the Eucharist at least during the Easter season.
- To observe the days of fasting and abstinence established by the Church.
- To help provide for the needs of the Church.

God loves you! God understands you. He has made a way for you to return to Him in the sacrament of Penance, the gift of reconciliation. Use this gift often, and rejoice in Jesus!

THE ANOINTING OF THE SICK

*They brought to him all who were sick with various diseases
and racked with pain, those who were possessed, lunatics,
and paralytics, and he cured them.*

MATTHEW 4:24

Jesus was the Word of God made flesh—the compassion of God for all, especially the sick, the sinful, and the marginalized.

The Gospels clearly teach that Jesus came to set us free, and to heal us in spirit, soul, and body. Jesus' healings were a sign that God's Kingdom was breaking forth into our world. His very name, *Yeshua*, means *God shall save*, and indeed Jesus came to heal us of our bondage to sin and all its effects—spiritual, physical, mental, and social.

Moreover, Jesus' healing was an attack on the kingdom of Satan (Cf. 1 John 3:8). In order to initiate the Kingdom, Jesus had to break the power of the Evil One and liberate people from his bondage. On the Cross Jesus totally and definitively overcame sin and death, a victory that is revealed now in the Church and will be fully revealed in the Parousia.

The greatest healing Christ offers us is salvation—the forgiveness of our sins and a new life—as a child of God, free of sin, and filled with the power of the Holy Spirit.

Pope Gregory the Great taught that miraculous healings were a foretaste of heaven and a sign of that union with God for which all believers are destined. He encouraged people to pray for healing through the intercession of Mary and the saints.

Humanity has long struggled with illness and suffering. Affliction can lead either to bitterness and despair or to a child-like trust in God, who is with us and has come to heal us. Jesus healed all who were brought to Him and gave His disciples healing power as well. Through the ages the Holy Spirit has poured out healing charisms to manifest Jesus' grace and peace.

The sacrament of the Anointing of the Sick confers a special grace of healing on the believer experiencing serious illness or old age. A priest administers this sacrament by anointing the forehead and hands of the sick person with blessed oil, and by laying his hands on the person and praying for God's healing grace.

This Anointing unites the sick to the Passion of Christ, for their good and that of the whole Church. It imparts strength, peace, and courage; it forgives sins, restores health if it is conducive to salvation, and prepares for their passing over into eternal life. In this final Passover, Mother Church accompanies her children to surrender them into the hands of their Compassionate Father, looking forward to their final Resurrection and eternal joy.

THE HISTORY OF THE ANOINTING OF THE SICK

*Is anyone among you sick? He should summon the presbyters
of the church, and they should pray over him and anoint [him]
with oil in the name of the Lord, and the prayer of faith will save
the sick person, and the Lord will raise him up.
If he has committed any sins, he will be forgiven.*

JAMES 5:14-15

The Acts of the Apostles clearly records how the disciples continued Jesus' work, preaching God's Word and performing many healings, signs, and wonders. Indeed, the early Church seemed to simply expect that it would carry on Jesus' ministry of healing and deliverance. In 1 Corinthians 12:9, Saint Paul includes healing as one of the gifts of the Holy Spirit, and Saint James specifically directs the elders to pray over the sick and to anoint them with oil for healing. Clearly, God's healing power was not limited to the earthly ministry of Jesus.

Saint Irenaeus, Saint Augustine, and many other leaders of the nascent Church attest to numerous miraculous healings and exorcisms occurring in their communities, often through the laying on of hands. The first official rite for anointing the sick appeared in the ninth century, inviting priests and laity alike to pray over and anoint the ill for both physical and spiritual healing.

As time passed, the use of the blessed oil was reserved only to clerics, and in time the rite of anointing became the final anointing—*Extreme Unction*—of someone who was dying. The purpose of the sacrament, for medieval theologians, was to prepare a person for a holy death and their entry into heaven. As such, the sacrament forgave all sin and also the sinful habits which might remain in a person. Secondly, this sacrament could bring about physical healing.

By the 13th century, the attitude toward healing was changing, due in part to Saint Thomas Aquinas, who asserted that the miracles of the early Church were done primarily to prove Christ's divinity and to validate His teaching. In our own day, theologians have helped us rediscover the New Testament understanding of the Anointing of the Sick: that God gave us this sacrament for physical and spiritual healing in *this* life, with a view toward recovery rather than impending death.

Since Vatican II, the emphasis of the revised rite is now on healing and making the person stronger. The ill can receive the Sacrament of Anointing as often as needed. Priests can anoint those with less serious illnesses either alone or communally. If this is indeed the final anointing of a person, the rite can be celebrated with Confession and Holy Communion.

The Anointing of the Sick is meant to be administered as part of a total ministry of care to the sick. The faithful can also serve the sick, especially by praying with the priest in this sacrament for the health and consolation of all those who seek healing.

PREPARATION FOR THE ANOINTING OF THE SICK

The Church invites any believer who is seriously ill or whose health is seriously impaired to receive the Anointing of the Sick. Understandably, this responsibility may fall to a family member or friend who either summons the priest to the home or hospital, or brings the sick person to church for the anointing. Sick call sets, which typically include a standing crucifix, blessed candles, and a holy water bottle, are available for those who receive the sacrament in their home.

People may receive the Anointing of the Sick repeatedly, if they recover after being anointed and then relapse, or if their condition worsens after the first anointing. If someone is going in for a serious surgery, he or she may likewise be anointed. The elderly can be anointed if they suffer from undue weakness even if a serious illness is not present. The Church anoints children who are sick, as long as they have sufficient use of reason to be strengthened by the sacrament. In case of doubt, the sacrament is still to be conferred.

God thus makes this sacrament available to His people, who should understand the meaning of this sacrament, ask for it, and prepare for it with heartfelt faith and sincere devotion. Obviously, someone who is unrepentant may not receive this sacrament, for God respects our free will. He will not force His presence, His forgiveness, nor his healing, on anyone.

HOLY VIATICUM

As we have noted, the Anointing of the Sick is God's gift to all who may suffer from serious illness or infirmity. Beyond that, it is His gift to those who are close to death, who are ready to depart this life and to come into His presence.

In such a case, the Church calls this the "*sacramentum exeuntium* (the sacrament of those departing)" (CCC 1523). Just as in Baptism, God began our transformation into Christ, so here He completes our conformity to His death and Resurrection.

The Church offers to those near death the Holy Eucharist as *Viaticum*, the final Eucharist someone receives after the Anointing of the Sick.

Viaticum is derived from the Latin word meaning provisions for the journey—in this case, the final journey from death into life. The Eucharist is the most precious gift anyone could ever receive as strength, comfort, confidence, and consolation for their final passage. This tradition dates back to Saint Justin Martyr, in the first century. The need for Viaticum led to the reservation of the Holy Eucharist in tabernacles, and hence we have the Blessed Sacrament always present in our Catholic churches, day and night. God is good beyond our expectation!

If the dying cannot take the Holy Eucharist in the host, under the form of bread, they may receive the Blood of Christ. "He who eats my flesh and drinks my blood has eternal life, and I will raise him up at the last day" (JOHN 6:54).

THE RITE OF THE
ANOINTING OF THE SICK

The sacrament of the Anointing of the Sick can be celebrated in different ways, as has been noted. It begins with a brief instruction followed by a Penitential rite and a reading from Scripture, for as Saint Paul notes, "Faith comes from what is heard, and what is heard comes through the word of Christ" (ROMANS 10:17).

The priest lays his hands on the sick person and prays silently for him or her. Again, this is in obedience to the injunction of Saint James. The priest then anoints the sick person with blessed oil. Ideally he would use the oil of the sick, known as the *Oil of the Infirm*, which is blessed by the bishop at the Chrism Mass every Holy Thursday.

When possible, it is best to celebrate this sacrament in community. In the case of a home visitation, the priest opens with a greeting of peace, and invites all to reflect on their own need of Our Lord's healing presence and power. He prays a brief prayer of penitence, and then offers a reading from Scripture and a brief homily. The assembly then prays a litany for the sick person, praying for him or her by name and asking God to strengthen, deliver, and free them from sin and temptation.

The priest lays his hands on the sick person's head and everyone joins him in silent prayer.

The priest anoints the person on the forehead, praying, "Through this holy anointing, may the Lord in His love and mercy help you with the grace of the Holy Spirit." All answer: "Amen."

He then anoints the tops of the hands, saying, "May the Lord who frees you from sin save you and raise you up." All answer: "Amen."

The priest prays a prayer after the anointing, and then everyone prays the Lord's Prayer together. The priest then offers the Eucharist to the sick person and anyone else who comes forward to receive Holy Communion. There is a period of silent prayer followed by a prayer after Communion, a final blessing, and dismissal.

THE EFFECTS AND FRUITS
OF THE ANOINTING OF THE SICK

Like any good mother, the Church is there for us at all stages of our life, from the womb to the tomb. She is there to wash us with the waters of Baptism that bring us into God's family, and to anoint us with the chrism which seals us as members of the Body of Christ. She feeds us with the Bread of Life in the Holy Eucharist and forgives our sins through the sacrament of Penance. She strengthens us with the gift of the Holy Spirit in Confirmation and blesses our vocations in the sacraments of Matrimony and Holy Orders. Finally, at the end of our journey, she offers us the Anointing of the Sick to help prepare us for our heavenly home.

The first effect of this sacrament, according to the Catholic Catechism, is a *particular* gift of the Holy Spirit (italics added). Jesus promised us He would send the Holy Spirit, who comes alongside us as an intercessor, advocate, and comforter. Thus in this first grace, the Holy Spirit Himself comes upon us to strengthen and impart to us Christ's peace and courage to help us deal with the trials of age and sickness, and ultimately, the challenge of impending death.

Jesus is so very merciful to us. He truly understands our weaknesses and wants very much to help us in our weaknesses and needs. Truly, beyond the grave, He has reserved delights unspeakable for those who love Him, but first we have to get there!

The particular gift of the Holy Spirit received in the Anointing of the Sick includes the forgiveness of sins for the penitent, especially if he confesses his sins as part of the ritual.

The next effect of this healing sacrament is union with the Passion of Christ. The anointing confers the strength and gift to unite ourselves more closely with Jesus in His suffering and death. The Church teaches that the sick person is, in a certain way, "consecrated to bear fruit by configuration to the Savior's redemptive Passion" (CCC 1221). God thus helps those who are anointed to accept their sufferings and join them to the suffering of Jesus for the sake of the whole world. Let us remember that Christ turns all suffering into Resurrection. He has already overcome, and He overcomes again in us.

The Anointing of the Sick also confers an "ecclesial grace." Those who unite their sufferings to Jesus' own Passion "contribute to the good of the People of God" (CCC 1522). The Church intercedes for her sick members, and they intercede for the Church and the salvation of all people. In God's economy, nothing is wasted.

In summary, the sacraments of Baptism, Confirmation, and Eucharist "initiate" us into our Christianity and our heroic pilgrimage. The sacraments of Penance and the Anointing of the Sick, including Viaticum, complete our pilgrimage and prepare us for the gift of heaven. To God be the glory!

THE SACRAMENT OF MATRIMONY

That is why a man leaves his father and mother and clings to his wife, and the two of them become one body.

GENESIS 2:24

Do you want to be happy? I do! God teaches us that we must then love as He loves, in "sincere self-giving." In the Marriage covenant a man and a woman enter into an intimate communion of life and love ordered to their good and to the generation and education of children. Jesus raised marriage to a sacramental dignity at the wedding in Cana. Marriage symbolizes Christ's faithful love for *His* Bride, the Church. It perfects the love of husband and wife, strengthens their unity, consecrates them, and makes them holy as they journey together to heaven (CCC 1601, 1613, 1617, 1638).

Discord, infidelity, and conflicts threaten marital unity, indissolubility, and openness to children. Without Christ, man and woman cannot achieve their God-ordained union. Thankfully, the Holy Spirit and the sacraments are ever available to help married couples renew and strengthen their love (CCC 1606-1608, 1624).

Divorce separates what God has joined together. Persons divorced from a living lawful spouse who choose to remarry objectively contravene God's plan and law. Though they cannot receive Eucharistic communion, they are joined to the Church and will lead Christian lives especially by educating their children in the faith (CCC 1650-1651).

It is in the home that faith is first proclaimed to children, the supreme gift of marriage. Our personal and societal well being is closely tied to a healthy conjugal and family life, an image of God's love for us that is not only good, but very good! (CCC 1603, 1652, 1666).

THE HISTORY OF MATRIMONY

*"For this reason a man shall leave (his) father and (his) mother
and be joined to his wife, and the two shall become one flesh."
This is a great mystery, but I speak in reference to Christ
and the church.*
EPHESIANS 5:31-32

Marriage has existed since the earliest times, as far as we can tell. It was arranged and performed through the family, and not through the religions of the day. Marriage was seen as a contract, or agreement, between families: more legalistic and less romantic! The fathers of each family agreed upon the terms, many of which dealt with property rights; they exchanged gifts, and often presided over the marriage ceremonial itself.

Hence Jesus did not institute the practice; however, He surely participated in many ceremonies in His hometown and dramatically intervened in the wedding feast at Cana in Galilee. (SEE JOHN 2:1-10). He later clarified God's original and unchanging intention for marriage, teaching that from the very beginning, "'God made them male and female. For this reason a man shall leave his father and mother (and be joined to his wife), and the two shall become one flesh.' So they are no longer two but one flesh. Therefore what God has joined together, no human being must separate" (MARK 10:6-9). Jesus adds, "I say to you, whoever divorces his wife (unless the marriage is unlawful) and marries another commits adultery" (MATTHEW 19:9).

Saint Paul also spoke of marriage, allowing that if a believer was married to an unbeliever and "the unbeliever separates, however, let him separate. The brother or sister is not bound in such cases; God has called you to peace" (1 CORINTHIANS 7:15).

During the early centuries of the Church, marriage continued to be a family matter. Priests and bishops at times did pray for and bless the new couples, but the Church did not have any ceremony *per se* to begin marriages. In the 4th century, Saint Augustine reiterated that, as a sign of Christ's love for the Church, marriage should be permanent. Even so, separation and divorce was debated and allowed in certain situations, even for believers.

In the societal confusion following the Fall of Rome and the rise of new cultures, bishops insisted that a priest must witness a marriage for it to be valid. This in turn necessitated special rites, and thus the nuptial Mass and ceremony was born.

The Council of Florence in 1439 listed marriage as an official sacrament, a visible sign of the love and union of Christ with His Body, the Church. The ends of marriage were procreation and the spiritual transformation of each spouse through the grace of the sacrament, their mutual support, and their physical union of conjugal love. The Council of Trent affirmed that God intended the bonds between husband and wife to be unbreakable, and clarified the Church's role in marriage as well. A valid marriage required a priest and two persons to witness the couple who "give" the sacrament to each other.

As society evolved, marriage evolved also, from a "social duty" to an individual right and from a "parental arrangement" to a personal choice. The Church has reflected much on the nature and sacramentality of marriage, culminating in the revisions of Vatican II, which speaks of marriage not so much as a contract involving property rights, but rather a covenant rooted deeply in Scripture; a divine and social institution, a union in love.

The bishops reasserted that the ends of marriage were procreation and the education of children. However, they also affirmed that spousal love was part and parcel in the development and transformation of the whole person. Both spouses are called to give fully of themselves in total fidelity to one another to bring about the intimate union of marriage and the good of their children. Thus marriage is God's call to holiness for all who enter into it.

The Council Fathers also revised the Rite of Matrimony, giving couples greater freedom in choosing their readings and vows, etc. In addition, they broadened the grounds for annulment of a marriage, including psychological and emotional reasons in their deliberation of the original validity of a marriage.

Marriage is not only for the good of the family, but of the Church itself. It is a sign of God's age-old for each of us, and a revelation of His plan to unite Himself with us in His Son Christ Jesus. Saint Paul reveals this to us in the fifth chapter, verses 21-28 of his letter to the Ephesians.

In this passage, Saint Paul urges us to be simultaneously subject to one another—in a mutual and sincere self-giving—out of reverence for Christ. He instructs wives to submit themselves to their husbands, whose mission it is to love their wives as Christ loved the Church and gave himself for her. God's Word calls wives to allow their husbands to serve them in a mutual service. Pope  John Paul further elucidates this by teaching that the husband must be the first to serve, as he is above all 'he who loves', and his wife is 'one who is loved.'

Saint Paul teaches us that this 'dying and rising' for one another will lead us to feel a deep and holy reverence for Christ in our hearts. The deep mystery of our sexuality, this awesome and vital gift of God, fills us with a holy fire, and we are transformed more and more into the image of Jesus himself. Not only that, as the Church, the Bride of Christ, we always need His love, ministered to us through the sacraments and in many other ways, to fill us, that we might be more intimately united with Him.

PREPARATION FOR MATRIMONY

Pope John Paul II observed that Matrimony serves in some ways as the model or 'prototype' of all the sacraments. This is because the Church is the Bride of Christ. God is preparing a bride for His Son, and our destiny is to be united with Christ our Bridegroom forever in the kingdom of heaven.

In addition to being a wonderful romantic experience, marriage is a most solemn undertaking, a life-changing decision, our unqualified "Yes!" to an unknown adventure of love and faith. Like any adventure, the better we prepare for it, the better chance we have for a successful outcome.

It's no secret that many marriages today, Catholic or otherwise, end in divorce. A multitude of challenges face married couples, including infidelity, addiction, a past history of abuse in the life of one or both partners, and our culture's contraceptive mentality. When you add dual careers, financial stresses, materialism, and the pervasive influence of individualism, it's clear that we need to help couples better prepare for marriage.

The first and best preparation for marriage is Jesus Himself living within us. We are able to love because He first loves us. Next would be the healthy love of a father and mother modeled for us. If we are blessed to be raised in such a family, we see how a husband and wife can love each other, forgive each other, work through trials and challenges together, and care for one another through the inevitable transitions of life.

Thankfully, God can heal and teach us even if we come from less than ideal homes. Often our own painful experiences of dysfunctional upbringing can spur us on to find healing for ourselves and learn ways to live and love more successfully.

In an effort to better prepare young people for marriage and to avoid marital meltdowns, many Catholic high schools, colleges, and parishes today provide courses on the theology of marriage, the theology of the body, and the practical, day-in and day-out aspects of marriage and family. The Diocese of Phoenix, Arizona, for example, requires couples seeking a church wedding to enter a nine-month preparation. During this time the future bride and groom receive a full course of instruction in Natural Family Planning, study together the theology of Christian marriage, and take a comprehensive course on the practical skills needed in marriage.

Fundamentally, marriage is about each partner being willing to give 100% of themselves to the other in self-donation. The only way we can do that is to allow Christ to love through us. He is the only one who can give totally of Himself. Thus marriage calls us first to receive God's love for us. This assurance that we are loved and that Jesus will never leave us fuels us to integrate all the other elements of preparation within ourselves so that we can approach the altar on our wedding day with confidence, hope, and joy.

"Love never fails."
1 CORINTHIANS 13:8

THE RITE OF MATRIMONY

Like many good things, the essence of the marriage rite is simple: the exchange of consent between two spouses. A priest or deacon and at least two other people must witness this exchange, receiving their consent in the name of the whole Body of Christ, and blessing the couple and their union.

Although the rite of Matrimony can be celebrated within the Liturgy of the Word, the Church encourages couples to celebrate their wedding within the Mass itself, which opens with the priest, servers, and groom entering the church sanctuary. There they await the entrance of the bridal party and the beautiful bride, escorted by her father. The readings chosen beforehand by the bride and groom reflect their own special love. The priest proclaims the Gospel and shares a homily filled with his encouragement and words of faith for the couple.

The actual rite of Matrimony begins then, with the bride and groom attesting to their free will in coming to give themselves in marriage. The celebrant asks the couple to join their right hands and to declare before God and the Body of Christ their intentions and consent.

The husband gives his consent first, vowing to take his beloved as his wife. He promises to serve her in the good times as well as the bad, in times of sickness and health. "I will love you and honor you all the days of my life." His bride then vows the same promises to him.

The celebrant affirms their consent, asking God's blessing on the newlyweds and reminding them, "What God has joined, men must not divide." At this point, the couple is married sacramentally, although of course the Mass and other traditional rituals continue!

The priest blesses the wedding rings and hands them to the spouses, who in turn offer their rings to one another as a sign of their "love and fidelity," in the name of the Father, and of the Son, and of the Holy Spirit. After the Lord's Prayer, the priest invites the entire congregation to join him in praying a special nuptial blessing over the couple. The blessing ends with the prayer that they live to see their grandchildren and someday enter the fullness of life with all the saints.

After Communion, the couple will often take a bouquet of flowers to Our Lady at her shrine in the church, praying for her motherly intercession in their married love. The priest then gives a final blessing, asking God for His special grace to strengthen, fortify, and unite the couple. He also prays for them to always be a blessing to others as well. Finally, he presents the newly married husband and wife to the assembly. Let the celebrating begin!

THE EFFECTS AND FRUITS OF MATRIMONY

The first effect of Matrimony is the marriage bond. This bond is by its very nature "perpetual and exclusive" according to the Catholic Catechism. The marriage bond springs from God's own nature and teaches us something about our Father. It's a covenant like the covenant He made with Israel and His New Covenant with us. God is faithful, and He has promised to ever keep His covenant with us and to be true to His word to us. Similarly, the marriage bond—the conjugal covenant—is irrevocable and indissoluble. It cannot ever be dissolved.

The sacrament of Matrimony also confers to the couple a special grace to strengthen and consecrate them for the duties and dignity of their wedded union. Jesus wants to be at the center of each marriage, just as He is the center of the universe and history itself, as Pope John Paul II stated in the opening sentence of his first encyclical, *Redemptor Hominis*. By virtue of the sacrament of Matrimony, spouses can draw ceaselessly on the love of Jesus present in their marriage to support and renew themselves in their vocation to love, honor, and serve one another and their families.

The Church teaches further that "authentic married love is caught up into divine love" (CCC 1639). God Himself calls the man and wife together, and in their conjugal embrace He weds them into one. He also has the power to keep them one, as they cooperate with His grace.

The grace which flows from the sacrament of Matrimony is meant to perfect and complete the couple's love and to strengthen their unity. This unity is an ongoing project! Through this grace the husband and wife help each other to grow in

holiness, to endure patiently the challenges and hardships of shared life, to forgive one another, to reverence each other, and to tenderly express their mutual love, which is a foretaste of the wedding feast of the Lamb in heaven.

In addition to unity and indissolubility, the sacrament of Matrimony calls the couple to be open to new life. Vatican II proclaimed, "Children are really the supreme gift of marriage and contribute very substantially to the welfare of their parents" (*Gaudium et Spes*, 50). Children are an obvious fruit of the covenant union between a husband and wife. Hence, openness to fertility is an essential element of the marriage vows.

The Christian home can also be seen as a fruit of marriage, for it is here where parents, the primary educators of their children, first proclaim their faith by their actions and later by their words. The family home is "the domestic church," a place where all can find true rest, true grace, shared prayer, and a place to grow, as Jesus did, in "wisdom and age and favor before God and man" (LUKE 2:52).

THE SACRAMENT OF HOLY ORDERS

*It was not you who chose me, but I who chose you
and appointed you to go and bear fruit that will remain,
so that whatever you ask the Father in my name he may give you.*

JOHN 15:16

God is always the Divine Initiator. He creates us from nothing;
He first loves us; He chooses us. Jesus brought us the
Kingdom, and He also invites us to share this Kingdom with
others, indeed with everyone. The sacrament of Holy Orders
and the sacrament of Matrimony are two ways He does this.

Holy Orders is the sacrament whereby Christ continues to
entrust His mission to men as He did to His apostles, that
they continue His work in the Church until His return in
glory. This sacrament of apostolic ministry has three orders, or
degrees: episcopate, presbyterate, and diaconate.

The first priest we see in the Scripture is the mysterious figure of Melchizedec, the king of Salem (CF. GENESIS 14:18-20), who offers bread and wine to God and blesses Abraham. Later, God chooses Aaron and his sons and the tribe of Levi to minister before Him and to offer sacrifice as priests of Israel.

Jesus' followers saw Him as a rabbi, a teacher, a prophet, and ultimately, the Messiah, but they did not see Him as a priest. Only later, as they reflected on His saving work at Calvary, did they begin to see that Jesus was both a priest who offered a sacrifice and a victim who became that sacrifice for our sake.

The Twelve Apostles went out after Pentecost teaching and preaching the Good News. They also shepherded the growing community of believers in and around Jerusalem. In time, they were joined by deacons (Greek: *diakonos*), elders (*presbyteros*), and overseers (*episkopos*). There was no set rule for passing on the authority and gifting of the Holy Spirit for these roles. Typically the apostles and other early leaders would choose believers of proven moral character and ability, and they would pray over them, and lay hands on—ordain—them for ministry. By the second century, the overseers (bishops) were in charge of the local churches, assisted by presbyters (priests) and deacons. After Constantine legalized Christianity, he allowed bishops to act as local civic leaders. The local church typically elected the bishop, who was ordained by neighboring bishops. He in turn, with his local presbyters, ordained new priests, while he alone ordained deacons, who primarily served through the bishop.

The diaconate as a separate ministry began to disappear in the fifth century, and was only preserved as a step—the transitional diaconate—toward priesthood. Around this time priests, influenced by monks, began to choose celibacy as a sign of their total commitment to the Lord.

As time passed, the clergy evolved into a separate class, a hierarchy, in the Church. Holy Orders was the name of the sacrament which empowered men to enter this ministry. As the Roman Empire crumbled, this disciplined and dedicated hierarchy stepped forth to help shepherd and bring order to a bewildered society. During the following centuries, Western civilization evolved into a temporal, feudal system of kings, lords, and peasants, and an eternal, spiritual system of popes, clergy, and laity. Oftentimes the two systems intermingled, with good and bad consequences.

The emphasis moved from ministry as service to ministry as authority and jurisdiction. New bishops received at their ordination a stole, ring, crosier, and miter as symbols of their authority. They in turn invested newly ordained priests with the symbols of their office: a chasuble and stole, chalice and paten.

Holy Orders traditionally included the major orders of deacon, priest, and bishop, as well as the minor orders of porter, lector, exorcist, and acolyte. The bishops at Vatican II revised the ordination ceremonies and approved the restoration of the permanent diaconate after more than a millennium. In 1972, Pope Paul VI suppressed the minor orders.

Thus, from the beginnings of the Church, there have been different degrees of ordained ministry. A bishop receives the fullness of the sacrament of Holy Orders. As a true and authentic teacher of the faith, he oversees a local church, or diocese. He guides the work of the Church locally, governs the faithful, and coordinates the ministries of the Body of Christ. He is called to be "a faithful overseer and guardian." Moreover, as successor of the apostles, a bishop is a member of the college of bishops and is called to be concerned for all the churches, as his diocese is organically part of the universal Catholic Church.

A priest is a co-worker with the bishop. He is called to be faithful to his ministry and to be a model of integrity. In a sense, a priest is the overseer of his particular parish, and he is charged to preach God's Word, to celebrate the Holy Sacrifice of the Mass, to administer the sacraments, and to nurture the growth of the parish, under the shepherding of his bishop.

Permanent deacons are ordained to serve (*diakonein*–to serve). A deacon is to be of good repute, filled with the Holy Spirit and wisdom. He assists the bishop, especially in the celebration of the Eucharist, and serves Jesus by serving others. Deacons proclaim the Gospel and may also preach at Mass. They may also baptize, witness and bless marriages, bring Viaticum to those in danger of death, and preside over funerals. Deacons are charged especially to minister to the poor, the sick, those in prison, and the oppressed. Deacons are a bridge, then, between the clergy and the laity, helping to motivate all to receive God's love and to serve Him as best they can.

THE RITE OF HOLY ORDERS

The presiding bishop of a diocese typically ordains new priests at the diocesan cathedral, in the company of the faithful, joined by a large number of his priests. After the Gospel the candidates are presented to the bishop, who invites them to come forward. He instructs all present on the meaning, rights, and responsibilities of ordination. After the candidates indicate their readiness to undertake their holy mission, they give their promise of respect and obedience to the bishop and his successors. The bishop concludes, "May God who has begun the good work in you bring it to fulfillment."

The candidates lie prostrate, face down on the floor while the community prays for them, intoning the Litany of the Saints.

The bishop imposes his hands on the candidates in silence, followed by all priests who are present, as a sign of their communion and solidarity with their new brothers. The bishop then solemnly consecrates the priests, asking God to grant them the dignity of priesthood and the Spirit of holiness.

Meanwhile, the bishop, parents, or priest mentors, invest the new priests each in a chasuble, the outer vestment worn at Mass. The bishop then anoints the hands of the priests with sacred chrism, praying that Jesus, whom the Father anointed with power in the Holy Spirit, would preserve them to sanctify their people and offer sacrifice to God. The bishop presents each of the new priests with a chalice and paten as symbols of the Eucharist they will now be able to offer. The bishop charges the priests to accept these gifts from God's people, to imitate the mystery they will celebrate, and to model their lives on the mystery of the Cross.

The bishop then gives the sign of peace to the new priests and invites all the priests present to embrace the newly ordained. At this time it is customary for the new priests to greet their parents, families, and friends with the sign of peace as well. They then join the bishop and other priests in concelebrating what truly is their "first Mass."

A bishop must consecrate a new bishop, assisted by at least two other bishops. An element of the ritual dating from the fifth century is the act of placing the open book of the Gospels over the new bishop's head during the act of consecration.

A deacon is ordained solely by a bishop, who lays his hands on the deacon-elect's head and prays a prayer of consecration. He then vests the deacon with a stole and dalmatic, and gives him the book of the Gospels. The newly ordained deacon then assists the bishop at the Mass.

THE FRUITS AND EFFECTS
OF HOLY ORDERS

Therefore, since we have a great high priest who has passed
through the heavens, Jesus, the Son of God, let us hold fast to our
confession. For we do not have a high priest who is unable
to sympathize with our weaknesses, but one who has similarly
been tested in every way, yet without sin.
HEBREWS 4:14-15

It is Jesus Himself, and He alone, who calls a person to participate in His own Priesthood. When a man receives the sacrament of Holy Orders as deacon, priest, or bishop, he is thus configured to Christ in a special way. Holy Orders enables him to act as a representative of Christ in His triple office of priest, prophet, and king. The sacrament of Holy Orders conveys an indelible spiritual character which is permanent and cannot be repeated.

It is possible, with papal approval, for a validly ordained minister to be laicized—dismissed from his priestly obligations and functions—but he can never undo what has been given to him. A bishop, priest, or deacon is marked forever by the vocation and mission received on his ordination day.

Holy Orders confers the gift of ministerial priesthood, which is a special grace and sacred power for the service of the Body of Christ. This power enables an ordained minister to teach, to lead or assist in divine worship, and to pastorally govern the people of God.

In Holy Orders, the Lord gives a bishop the grace of strength to govern his people, to guide and defend them with fortitude and prudence, with love for all, especially the poor, the sick, and the needy. This spirit impels him to preach the Gospel, to lead his flock, "identifying himself in the Eucharist with Christ the priest and victim, not fearing to give his life for his sheep" (CCC 1585).

Similarly, in the sacrament of Holy Orders, a priest receives the grace to stand before the Lord's altar, to proclaim the Gospel, to fulfill the ministry of the Word, and to offer gifts and sacrifices unto the Lord. The priest is empowered as a coworker with his bishop to renew God's people. When Christ returns, His shepherds will receive a loving reward for their faithful stewardship.

Holy Orders confers on a deacon the strength to dedicate himself to the people of God in union with the bishop and priests, "in the service (diakonia) of the liturgy, of the Gospel, and of works of charity" (CCC 1588).

God thus chooses these men to share more closely in His being, which is why we call a priest an *alter Christus*—another Christ. It is from this interior identification with Christ and love for Him that the priest is empowered and inspired to offer his own sacrificial gift of himself to the Lord for the sake of His Body, the Church.

JESUS, THE SACRAMENT OF GOD

*And the Word became flesh
and made his dwelling among us.*
JOHN 1:14

A sacrament is a sign, an outer ritual that conveys an inner grace. Thus those who receive a sacrament in faith experience a divine encounter. The Catholic Catechism states that **"Christ himself** is the mystery of salvation. ... **The saving work of his holy and sanctifying humanity** is the sacrament of salvation, which **is revealed and active in the Church's sacraments** ..." (CCC 774).

We can imagine that each person who heard Jesus preach, saw Him heal, or felt His touch, had a personal encounter with the Lord—veiled in His humanity—yet a very real experience, nonetheless. Jesus' contemporaries watched Him stretch out His hands to heal the sick, bend down to listen to children, fearlessly stand up for the truth against his antagonists, and lovingly forgive repentant sinners like the woman caught in adultery. If they were at all open, Jesus filled their hearts with His love and the awareness that they were no longer alone—that God was with them!

Jesus was Himself the sacrament of God for His people. He was both the presence of God and the one who communicated that presence to others. No wonder people wanted to be around Jesus! They all felt loved!

THE CHURCH: SACRAMENT OF CHRIST

You are the light of the world.
MATTHEW 5:14

Saint Augustine said that a sacrament is a visible sign of an invisible reality. Christ Jesus is the *invisible reality*, the only-begotten Son of God who became flesh and lived among us as a man. He died, arose from the dead, and ascended in heaven, and now the *visible sign* of Christ is His Body, the Church. **We, the Body of Christ, are *the sacrament of Christ!***

Jesus died to save all humanity—every human being ever created, from the beginning of the world until its end. He sent the Holy Spirit upon the infant Church at Pentecost to empower His followers to be His witnesses and bring His Gospel of the Kingdom "to the ends of the earth" (Acts 1:8). This Church is His Body, "the universal sacrament of salvation" (*Lumen Gentium*, p. 48). Jesus "lives forever to make intercession" for all who approach God through Him (Hebrews 7:25). He is continually at work leading people to the Church and through the Church, bringing them more deeply into communion with Himself.

The Vatican II Fathers remind us that Christ has already begun the restoration we have all longed for since the Fall of our first parents in the Garden of Eden. He carries this work forward through His Holy Spirit in us, His Body on earth. Thus the Church is the sacrament of Christ, the sacrament of His salvation for all.

A good analogy might be a stained glass window. As the brilliant sunlight pours through the window, it illuminates the room and touches all upon whom it falls. The window is not the source of the light, but it is the conduit. That being said, the light we experience is somehow a mix of the sunlight and the window through which it comes.

In a similar fashion, each one of us is called to allow Christ, the Light of the world, to shine through us. We need to first allow Jesus to touch us, to warm us, and to illumine us with His light. Then, suffused with His presence, we are called to allow Christ to shine His light through us to touch others through our words of faith, witness of hope, and works of love.

As the Body of Christ, each of us is united with Christ who is the Vine, and we are also united with one another—the branches! His Holy Spirit flows in and through us all as a Body; and the whole is much more powerful than any one member.

Hence, when a Catholic chaplain prays for victims of a natural disaster, bringing them comfort and peace, he, representing the Church, is a sacrament of Christ. When a nun in a far off country gathers poor children around her to feed and care for them and teach them about Jesus, she is a sacrament of Christ. When a mother stops to dry the tears of a child lost in a grocery store, she, representing the Church, is a sacrament of Christ. When a father takes a homeless man out for a good dinner and a compassionate visit, he is a sacrament of Christ. As Saint Teresa of Avila said, "Christ has no other hands but yours."

A FINAL WORD

From time immemorial, two bodies of water have existed in the Holy Land. In the north, the Sea of Galilee receives fresh water constantly from the Jordan and empties it out down towards the south. The Sea is teeming with life—24 varieties of fish, lush shrubbery and vegetation, and animals of all sorts along its banks. It is here where Jesus did most of His ministry.

To the south, there is another sea, that lies 1400 feet below sea level, and whose water is 35% salt. There are no fish, no animals, and no plants anywhere in or around this sea. This sea has no outlet; it does not pass the fresh waters of the Jordan along beyond its banks. It is aptly named the Dead Sea.

One sea gives, and lives; the other only takes, and dies. So it is with us. We must first receive God's life, if we are to truly live. We must *choose* to receive the sacraments, to go to Confession and Mass regularly, to receive God's forgiveness, His Word, and His Body and Blood, to spend time with Him in prayer.

Jesus calls us to then give what we've received—by serving others, listening to them, forgiving them, feeding and clothing the needy, cheering up the sick, and visiting the lonely. If we do this, we shall truly live, our waters will be fresh and life-giving, and God shall be glorified. Amen. Alleluia!

"Let the one who thirsts come forward,
and the one who wants it receive the gift of life-giving water."
REVELATION 22:17